DEATH POET'S WHORE

t. kilgore splake
25214 ash street
calumet, mi 49913
splake@chartermi.net

\# \# \# \#

ISBN: 978-1-946460-67-7

DEATH POET'S WHORE

t. kilgore splake
25214 ash street
calumet, mi 49913
splake@chartermi.net

# # # #

Publisher's Introduction
Dustin Pickering

With the cleverest irony of the Creator, I am listening to the Grateful Dead as I compose this introduction following a reading of the new splake creation. Speaking of irony, this particular batch of poems strikes me as having more subtle ironies within its pages than some past collections of splake's reflections.

My own poetry is riddled with thoughts of death lately. Some may consider this teen-angsty, and oddly my Instagram feed is filled with Nirvana clips. splake's latest celebration of life offers memories about Country music legends. Music is a strange thing and can speak for us when we are at our weakest. The suggestion of old-timey Country legends says something more serious about the poet than his preferences: that he feels close to death. Death is an ever-present reality for the graybeard poet whose reminiscences are instilled with irony and thoughtfulness. The criticism of those who fail to live the creative life when called is still part of splake's legacy.

All of his readers know splake's story. His poetry career begins with death and ends with it as well. This volume even offers its own Creation myth, ironic it is:

> "in the beginning
>
> god created heaven and earth
>
> today people staring in phone screens
>
> trying to find wisdom in light"

Everyone is valuable. Our presence on earth is timeless and unforgettable. However, the contemporary generation seems content to waste life in digital ecstasy. Are they seeking knowledge or distraction? Among these poems, we hear the graybeard poet searching his soul for meaning and purpose like many teens seek independence. Poetry, written in solitude, is also speaking in solitude. The dialogue with one's soul is precious.

Re-creating worlds is the art of art itself. We of the creative persuasions know too well what death says of creativity. Death, an arbitrary and delinquent muse, is untimely and strikes at our roots.

5

death poet's whore

serious poets always lost
in deep emotional shadows
surrounded by darkness
living on creative edge
with haunting empty feelings
frequently thinking of death
quietly ending lives
yet after killing themselves
many praying for afterlife
finding soul in heaven
living with angels
sitting beside god
they don't really believe

# # # #

we stopped at perfect days

leaving favorite brautigan poem in library books
waiting for surprised readers to discover wisdom
'it was as simple as that'

# # # #

thorazine shuffle

teenage girl refusing to take shrinker's drugs
believing with medicine she lost creative edge
destroyed new ideas for art

# # # #

freedom

beyond winnebagos in paved parking lots
diorama brief histories and creosote trail markers
well traveled hiking paths

# # # #

stranger in strange land

graybeard stepfather with new teenage daughter
learning about her books music movies and friends
understanding and encouraging young girl's dreams

# # # #

porcupine mountains eulogy

believe visiting wilderness would help depressed lover
however discovering nature cannot solve sad woman's problems
sadly preferring to be unhappy rather than becoming free

# # # #

shadows of bolero

continuous power of heart's passions
like after concert's performance over
music still echoing across brain

# # # #

lost dreams

watching morning coffee shop customers
blank faces lost in quiet distant stare
wondering if lives what they wanted

# # # #

sadness after failure

husband wanting to say "let's start over again"
instead cold bodies silently next to each other in bed
waiting lawyers divorce and alcoholic madness

# # # #

satisfaction

following near-death ecstasy
woman praying night would never end
body fucked cum leaking from wet cunt

# # # #

watermelon sugar dreams

richard brautigan's ghost visiting library every day
reading books on trout fishing and better bowling techniques
doing google search for 'ideath' and 'forgotten works'

# # # #

kingston plains forest graveyard

late night wind blowing through tree tops dream
music of axes crosscut saws and cries of tim-b-e-r
vanishing mornings on dark pine stump shadows

# # # #

being

escaping civilization by visiting brautigan creek
during brief moment alone in wilderness silence
becoming wind bird song wildflowers flowing water

# # # #

artist remote location

real estate prices cheap and property taxes low
every small town has splendid coffee shop for poet to write
computer connections to anywhere in the world

# # # #

genesis

in the beginning
god created heaven and earth
today people staring in phone screens
trying to find wisdom in light

# # # #

natural high

walking alone through forest
listening to pine trees hum
soft music of stream flowing
floating in wilderness poem
rising beyond clouds

# # # #

beyond unknown

most beautiful wilderness locations
require successful challenge to visit and enjoy
danger lost in seeking hidden forest secrets
facing death climbing to mountain summit
always moving beyond boundary limits

# # # #

poet looking beyond

artist's mind completely empty
no imagination or new creative dreams
desperately turning to religion
asking god to stop his fear of death
soul quietly disappearing

# # # #

lightness of being

tranny full of gas styrene coffee cups on console
turning highway miles with mind free to think
stopping long nighttime journey
after reaching dark rocky mountain shadows
having truckstop breakfast before turning around
quietly heading back home feeling free

# # # #

brautigan creek funeral

early morning rainbow shining through cliffs
mountain lions butterflies birds deer and rainbow trout
silently waiting in dark wilderness shadows
softly whispering quiet prayer
saying goodbye to warm forest poet friend
soul silently drifting away

# # # #

graybeard poet

wisdom gained from growing older
choosing comfort over elegance and style
wearing jeans t-shirts and old leather shoes
instead of shopping for latest clothing fashions
not needing cosmetic enhancements
satisfied with aging body and wrinkled skin
botox and creams for others

# # # #

running on empty

desperate artist
with nothing left in mind
facing possible decisions
finger on gun trigger
overdosing with pills
drowning in alcohol
finally leaving earth
never saying goodbye

# # # #

creative seasons

ice out coming into spring
wilderness pregnant with fresh life
while single wrinkled autumn leaf
remaining on tree branch
not victim of fall decay
silent reminder of graying poet
waiting creative activity
one more year

# # # #

soul

love never for sale
no dollars and cents
for successful business operation
emotions not expecting
anything in return
except continuously giving
sadly realizing most people
will never find it in their lives
sharing warm passions with another

# # # #

lost polaroid memories

smiling birthday child with cake and candles
teenage girl in prom dress with orchid
hospital nursery baby picture
tan lake swimming suit bodies
cap and gown graduate holding diploma
boys in t-shirts beside muscle cars
naked husband and wife in bedroom shadow
father's silent stare funeral home casket
blurry photo hiding life's failures

# # # #

almost one more once

early morning reflections
poet musing over past marriages
gayle's lacy dress wyandotte church service
caryl after work at vicksburg justice of peace
olga july afternoon in upper peninsula judge's home
somehow young jennifer having escaped wedding
before graybeard poet becoming stepfather
living with young pre-teen daughter

# # # #

poet's funeral

sunny late afternoon
dark cliffs shadows
beside brautigan creek
poet's final eulogies
soft pine needles hum
bird's gentle melodies
light forest breeze
rustling leaves and wildflowers
peaceful rippling flow
of stream waters
end of service
final wilderness silence

# # # #

end of creativity

poet seeking
new artistic inspiration
reading tarot cards
doing i-ching
ouiji board answers
nightly bedroom prayers
zen meditation
long mmm chanting
instead choosing
goddamn carpe diem
facing blank page

# # # #

creative reality

poet lost in writing sonnets and haikus
obeying fixed literary forms and rules
poems rhyming with so many lines
like pleasures of masturbation
pulling cock and rubbing clit
instead of capturing true human emotions
with lover done me wrong songs
hank williams and patsy cline
country and western prose poetry music
"your cheatin' heart" and "crazy"
telling what it really is

# # # #

creative life existentials

graybeard poet's reflections
after first early morning coffee
swallowing over dozen pills
painful arthritic body
slowly moving to bathroom
long piss emptying bladders
solving prostate problem
looking at mirror's familiar face
now frequently forgetting
names and faces of close friends
quietly living alone
waiting life's end

# # # #

growing up free

trooper ticketing poet for seat belt violation
officer using cop talk vocabulary
expert sounding law enforcement knowledge
vehicle instead of car
ammunition rather than bullets
firearms not guns
rigid personal attitudes
overblown sense of authority
wondering if policemen talk
like this in real life
over morning breakfast table
while playing with son and daughter
naked nights in bedroom shadows

# # # #

poet's dream

mutli-choice new girlfriends
divine angel mate
early morning bartender
graveyard shift waitress
neighbor's teenage daughter
rehabbing partner
stripper and lap dancer
tarot card reader
demon lilith or kali
country western singer
shy college student poet
maybe just a little bit
from all of the above

# # # #

artist's obituary

graybeard poet silent passing

ghost missing michigan football

saturday games at the big house

also not having right words

leaving empty crossword puzzle space

no wrigley field bleacher seats

drinking beer with wind blowing out

or watching green celtic uniforms

scoring boston parquet three pointers

missing special magic

successfully writing new poems

plus vanilla perfume scent

of beautiful young woman

still dearly loved

# # # #

bardic reflections

definite moments shape person's life
time before tom smith college professor
followed by becoming poet t. kilgore splake
trading burned out teaching frustrations
for new exciting writing adventure
suffering serious period of artistic block
afraid never writing anything serious again
dark depression during munising years
now achieving modest creative success
having long passed younger wildest dreams
graying senior's life rapidly disappearing
no longer worrying what literary critics say
poetic voice and vision totally free
because now who the fuck cares

# # # #

finding last romance

woman dating older men
who possess more maturity
survived emotional losses
remembering rock and roll
elvis chuck berry fats domino
also warm memories
of friendly bars that closed
trophy room and victory bar and grill
living through ex-wives deaths
gayle caryl and olga
after successfully weathering
life's shit happenings
quietly patient with me
holding naked body close
in afterglow of love making
softly whispering
you make me happy
really needing you

# # # #

graybeard bardic wisdom

important creative activity
artist should frequently listen
to simon and garfunkel
"slow down you move too fast
you got to make the morning last"
coltrane's saxophone "love supreme"
in "psalm" his voice softly singing
"its been sometime since i got high
on breathin' air without a care"
reverend martin luther king
looking forward to saying
"thank god almighty
we are free at last"
words and musical lyrics
reflecting need for artistic freedom
writers painters composers
being unafraid to create
because of others opinions
always waking mornings
continuing to see clearly

# # # #

mantra in motion

early morning jogger
ear buds tightly fixed
listening to heavy metal
loud music deafens thinking
outdoor running habits
providing satisfactory excuse
treadmill exercise never dull
graybeard poet daily logging
machine minutes and miles
running to brautigan creek
below cliffs shadows
leaving ash street bard res'
moving down pine street
passing copper island printers
publisher of writer's books
keweenaw auto body shop
place for frequent truck repairs
petersen's funeral home
where body will be cremated
turning north on m-26
past centennial mine frame
hut restaurant parking lot
down the hill into allouez
past "last place on earth"

tom and jan manniko's store

turning off on cliff drive

continuing wilderness miles

moving beyond

seneca lake and gratiot river

vanishing in shadows

finally reaching two-tire track

crossing brautigan creek

trail leading to cliffs summit

grabbing quick breath

resting for brief moment

before heading back home

traveling through eagle river

passing phoenix location

old copper mining remains

reaching metrops city limits

morning workout done

# # # #

www.ingramcontent.com/pod-product-compliance
Lightning Source LLC
Chambersburg PA
CBHW020957030426
42339CB00011B/87